What Is the Story of Alice in Wonderland?

What Is the Story of Alice in Wonderland?

by Dana Meachen Rau

illustrated by Robert Squier

Penguin Workshop

For the curious, strong, and fearless women
of my writers' group—Alices all—DMR

For Jessica, who appreciates books
with pictures and conversations—RS

PENGUIN WORKSHOP
An Imprint of Penguin Random House LLC, New York

The publisher does not have any control over and does not assume any responsibility for author or third-party websites or their content.

Sir John Tenniel's illustrations for *Alice's Adventures in Wonderland* and *Through the Looking-Glass and What Alice Found There*, which are in the public domain, appear on the following pages: 25, 31–39, 42–44, 49–59.

Visit us online at www.penguinrandomhouse.com.

Library of Congress Cataloging-in-Publication Data is available upon request.

ISBN 9781524791766 (paperback)   10 9 8 7 6 5 4 3 2 1
ISBN 9781524791773 (library binding)   10 9 8 7 6 5 4 3 2 1

Contents

What Is the Story of Alice in Wonderland?

On July 4, 2015, residents of and visitors to Oxford, England, were invited to a dance called the Lobster Quadrille. They gathered in a large grassy field. When the music began, they danced the steps they had been practicing for weeks. Adults and children dressed as lobsters, turtles, playing cards, white rabbits, and queens. Many wore blue dresses and white aprons to look like the seven-year-old character Alice from the book *Alice's Adventures in Wonderland*.

Every year, the town of Oxford presents Alice's Day to celebrate the day in July 1862 when the writer Charles Dodgson took three young sisters of the Liddell family on a boat ride up the river Thames. During the trip, he invented a story about a girl named Alice who enters a magical place filled with odd creatures, silly games, and ridiculous adults. After that boat ride, Charles wrote down his story and published it as a children's book.

But the celebration of Alice's Day in 2015 was extra special. The year 2015 marked 150 years since the publication of the book. The day was full of silly and strange events. Guests enjoyed tea parties and ran races that had no winners.

They acted out stories and solved riddles. They gazed at the bones of an extinct dodo (a bird that couldn't fly) at a nearby  museum and asked advice from a caterpillar. Leaves, clocks, and hats hung as decorations above the city's streets.

When the writer Charles Dodgson created Alice in the 1860s, many stories for children were written to provide life lessons, or to teach children to mind their manners. But Alice was not like the characters in most other children's books. She asked lots of questions, spoke up whenever she felt she should, often didn't follow the rules, and got into plenty of trouble.

Alice is so popular because she is curious, strong, and fearless, even when the world around her seems difficult to understand. Readers loved Alice when she first appeared in the book more than 150 years ago. She still has many fans throughout the world.

CHAPTER 1
Serious and Silly Charles Dodgson

Charles Lutwidge Dodgson was born on January 27, 1832, in Daresbury, England. His father worked for the church in the small village, and his mother took care of the home and children. Charles was the third oldest of eleven children.

Charles Lutwidge Dodgson

Charles's mother and father taught him and his siblings school lessons at home. There was also time for fun. Charles liked to entertain his younger brothers and sisters. He invented games, played with puzzles, and created tiny furniture for the Dodgson children's dollhouse. He used a wheelbarrow as a train to take riders to stops around the Dodgsons' garden.

Charles also loved to write. He made books of his own poems and homemade magazines to share with his family. He performed puppet shows with scripts he had written himself. One of the reasons he may have loved writing so much was because he had a stutter. It was difficult for him to say certain sounds. Writing was a way to get past that.

At age twelve, Charles left home for school, and he did very well in his subjects. He mostly enjoyed math and writing. His next step was college.

Charles entered Christ Church, a college of Oxford University, in 1851. He did so well at math that by the time he completed his studies in 1855, the college asked him to be a math teacher there. Charles was pleased to start a career at Oxford.

Christ Church, Oxford University

As a teacher, though, Charles wasn't the silly entertainer he had been at home. His students described him as stiff, shy, and dull! But when Charles sat at his writing desk, his personality was very different. He wrote stories and poems filled with humor and wordplay. Some of his work was published in magazines and newspapers. He made up a pen name for his writings. Instead of signing them *Charles Dodgson*, he called himself Lewis Carroll.

Education in Victorian England

Queen Victoria

The time period between 1837 and 1901 in the United Kingdom (England, Wales, Scotland, and Northern Ireland) is called the Victorian era. During these years, Queen Victoria ruled England. The country grew powerful and wealthy under her reign.

When Victoria became queen, not all children went to school. Poor children worked to earn money for their families. In wealthy families, a hired servant called a governess taught children at home. When boys reached age ten, they could go to school. Girls continued to receive lessons at home because there were not many schools for them.

Queen Victoria supported many positive innovations in England, such as inventions, transportation, and opportunities for work. One such positive change was an 1870 law that required all children, rich or poor, to attend school from ages five to ten. Schools opened all over England. That made it possible for all children to have the same basic education.

Writing wasn't Charles's only creative hobby. He also liked photography. Early in 1856, he got his own camera and took lots of pictures around the college to practice his picture-taking skills. One day in April, he wanted to take a picture of Oxford's cathedral from the garden of the dean's house. A new dean (a head of the college) had just moved in. Dean Henry George Liddell and his wife, Lorina, had two sons, Harry and Arthur, and three daughters, Lorina, Alice, and Edith. When Charles knocked on the door of the

deanery (the house where the dean and his family lived), he met three-year-old Alice for the first time. Neither of them knew it yet, but Alice Pleasance Liddell would be the inspiration for one of the most memorable children's characters in history.

Wet-Plate Photography

Taking pictures in the mid-1800s was not as quick and easy as it is today! Wet-plate photography was brand-new.

To take a picture using the wet-plate method, the photographer first had to clean and polish a flat pane of glass, then pour a thick syrup of chemicals over it. After that, in a darkroom, the glass was dipped into even more chemicals.

This glass pane—or plate—was placed inside a large wooden boxlike camera. Light entered through a lens for a few minutes. If the photograph was of a person, the subject had to sit perfectly still for the entire time, or the picture would come out blurry.

In a darkroom (or tent if outside), the photographer would wash the plate with even more chemicals until an image appeared, and then use the plate to print copies of the image on paper.

It was easy to make mistakes, so becoming a good photographer in the 1850s took a lot of time and practice.

Charles became good friends with the Liddell family. The boys had gone off to school, but the girls spent their time at home under the care of their governess, Miss Mary Prickett.

Miss Prickett

Charles visited the girls often. He liked to entertain them as he had his own siblings growing up.

Charles often brought toys, puzzles, and

games for the Liddell girls. They also posed for his photographs. The girls would dress up in playful clothes, and Charles would take pictures of them.

When the sisters visited Charles in his Oxford apartment, he would make up tales on the spot and draw little pictures to go with them.

Detail of a picture drawn by Charles Dodgson

In the summer months, he took them on outdoor trips. They often rowed boats together on the river Thames. The girls enjoyed having a grown-up to play with. And Charles was a grown-up who sometimes didn't seem to want to grow up at all!

CHAPTER 2
A Strange and Adventurous Story

On July 4, 1862, Charles Dodgson and his friend Robinson Duckworth invited the Liddell sisters—Lorina (then age thirteen), Alice (ten),

and Edith (eight)—on a trip up the river Thames. They loaded a big picnic basket into a boat near Folly Bridge. The men rowed for a few miles, and then they stopped near the town of Godstow to enjoy their picnic along the bank of the river.

The girls begged Charles: "Tell us a story." Making it up as he went along, Charles named the main character Alice, after Alice Liddell. He told a tale about a girl who follows a white rabbit down a hole and enters a strange world where nothing makes sense! The girls were delighted by Charles's wild adventure. At the end of the day, Alice Liddell told Charles that he had to write down the story. She didn't want to forget it.

In his diary four months later, in mid-November 1862, Charles wrote: "Began writing the fairy-tale for Alice—I hope to finish it by Christmas." But it actually took him about two years to write it. He used some parts of the story he had told during their picnic. He also added new ideas. In his rooms at Oxford, Charles handwrote the story and drew his own pictures for it. He collected his pages in a little handmade book with a green cover and called it *Alice's Adventures Under Ground*. He gave it to Alice as a gift to remember their special day.

Charles wondered whether other children would like his Alice story. He shared a copy with George MacDonald, a friend of his who wrote fairy tales. When MacDonald's six-year-old son, Greville, heard the story, he declared that there should be sixty thousand copies of it! MacDonald told Charles he thought the book should be published.

The handmade book, *Alice's Adventures Under Ground*, only had four chapters. Charles thought the story should be longer. He imagined new characters and scenes. His final version had twelve chapters. Charles also decided that the book would look better if the pictures were drawn by a professional artist. His friend Robinson Duckworth suggested the famous illustrator John Tenniel.

Charles told John Tenniel how big each illustration should be and where it should be placed in the story. But Tenniel didn't like to be told what to do. The two men argued over their different ideas. In the end, Tenniel drew Alice as a neat and proper Victorian girl in a stiff dress, apron, and little black shoes. His illustrations were filled with lots of weird and wonderful details.

Sir John Tenniel (1820–1914)

John Tenniel was an English artist who taught himself to draw by copying illustrations of costumes and armor from museum books. He also visited the zoo and drew pictures of animals.

Tenniel developed a cartoon style that was perfect for his work for a British humor magazine called *Punch.* Cartoons were often meant to be funny by exaggerating a character's features. Tenniel spent more than fifty years of his career at *Punch.*

Tenniel also drew pictures for books. The illustrations that he created for *Alice's Adventures in Wonderland* made him a world-famous artist during his lifetime. Queen Victoria even knighted him, giving Tenniel the title of Sir in 1893 to honor him and his work.

The London publisher Alexander MacMillan agreed to publish the book. Charles wanted to give it a new name. In a letter to his friend Tom Taylor on June 10, 1864, he shared a few of his ideas:

Alice's Golden Hour
Alice Among the Goblins
Alice's Hour in Wonderland
Alice's Doings in Elf-Land
Alice's Adventures in Wonderland

Of all of these possible titles and more, he liked *Alice's Adventures in Wonderland* the best. To this, he added his pen name: Lewis Carroll.

Charles sent Alice Liddell her own copy of the finished book on July 4, 1865—exactly three years after their picnic on the river. He didn't see the Liddell family—which eventually grew to include five more children—as much as he used

to. Alice was by then a young teenager, and not much like the seven-year-old character that she had inspired. But she would always be special to Charles.

Alice's Adventures in Wonderland, by Lewis Carroll, was released in late 1865, just in time for Christmas. Charles Dodgson hoped readers would like the curious girl he had created.

CHAPTER 3
A Very Curious Girl

Alice's Adventures in Wonderland begins with Alice and her older sister sitting under a tree along a river. Her sister is reading a book, but Alice is bored. The hot day makes her feel lazy and sleepy. Suddenly, a white rabbit rushes past. It's no ordinary rabbit. It wears a coat like that of an English gentleman and is looking at a pocket watch! The rabbit rushes into a hole under the bushes. Alice is a very curious girl—she crawls right in after him.

Soon, Alice starts falling. The fall takes so long that she's afraid she might be going all the way through the earth. In fact, so much time goes by, she gets bored again. She starts thinking about her geography lessons. She even starts missing her cat, Dinah, who is sure to miss her, too.

When Alice finally lands, she discovers a long hallway of locked doors. She worries about how she will ever get home! But she is also determined to find a way. She discovers a key on a small table and tries every lock. It works on a tiny door.

She is much too large to fit through it, but she peeks in and sees a beautiful garden on the other side.

A small bottle appears on the table labeled "Drink Me." When Alice drinks from the bottle, she starts to shrink. She can fit through the door.

But it has locked again, and she can't reach the key that she left on the table. She finds a cake with the words "Eat Me." When she eats the cake, she grows so tall that she can hardly see her feet. Alice is so frustrated that she starts to cry.

She cries so much that when she shrinks again, she slips and falls into a huge pool of her own tears. She meets a whole group of animals— a mouse, a duck, a dodo bird, and others—that have fallen into the pool.

Even though Alice is very confused about the strangeness of this new place, she still tries to act like a proper young lady. She uses her best manners, but the other characters don't seem to have any manners, or sense, at all! In fact, they are ridiculous. The dodo suggests they run a race to dry off. Everyone runs around in crazy ways, and no one wins. Alice tries to start a conversation about how much she loves her cat, but the mention of cats scares her new friends away.

The White Rabbit rushes past again and orders Alice to fetch his gloves and fan. Once inside his house, she drinks from another small bottle. This time, she grows so large that she fills the house.

Alice is enjoying living in a fairy tale, but she worries she'll be stuck in the house forever. The White Rabbit and his servants try to get her out by throwing pebbles at her. Lucky for her, the little rocks turn into cakes. Eating one makes her small again, and she runs out the door to escape.

But the silliness is not over! Alice's adventures continue with even more twists and turns. The grasses and flowers now look like a forest to tiny Alice. She comes upon a mushroom with a blue caterpillar sitting on top. In a sleepy voice,

he asks Alice many confusing questions. And she finally discovers something useful: If she eats a piece of the mushroom from one side, she grows taller—and taking a bite from the other side makes her smaller. She at last returns to her normal size. But this world is anything but normal!

Next Alice finds the Duchess—a rude and frightening woman. The Duchess hands Alice her sobbing and grunting baby, who turns into a pig and trots off! She also meets the mysterious grinning Cheshire Cat. He tells Alice,

"We're all mad here." (*Mad* is another word for crazy.) He sends her in the direction of a Mad Tea Party. Then he slowly disappears, leaving his toothy smile behind.

At the tea party, the Mad Hatter, the March Hare, and the Dormouse sit around a large table with many empty seats, but still they cry, "No room! No room!" Alice is confused by their riddles, stories, and songs. She rushes off through a door in a tree, and then she finds herself back in the long hallway of doors.

She takes the key off the table, and nibbles a bit of mushroom until she is just the right height. Then she goes through the tiny door into the beautiful garden she had been hoping to get into all along.

The garden, however, belongs to the Queen of Hearts, and she, and all her attendants, look like a deck of cards come to life. Everyone is afraid of the Queen. She roars in anger and threatens to chop off everyone's head.

Mad as a Hatter

Charles Dodgson may have chosen the character of a hatter (someone who makes hats) for his tea party because of the phrase "mad as a hatter." In Victorian times, hats were an important part of both men's and women's fashions. Many hats were formed from a type of fabric called felt. When making felt, the hatters had to soak it

in a chemical mixture that contained the metal mercury. After being exposed to mercury for too long, they could become sick. If a hatter came down with mercury poisoning, he might shake, have trouble speaking, and imagine things that weren't really there. This led people to believe that hatters were crazy because they couldn't seem to control themselves. The saying "mad as a hatter" became a common phrase.

The Queen orders Alice to play croquet. Alice is familiar with this game—she knows how to use a mallet to hit wooden balls through hoops stuck in the ground. But this game of croquet is so different! The ball is a curled-up hedgehog, and the mallet is a flamingo that won't keep still!

The Queen sends Alice to meet the Gryphon and the Mock Turtle, who tell her what school is like under the sea. They also describe a wonderful dance called the Lobster Quadrille, and they practice it together. But Alice has to cut her good time short to hurry back to the palace for a court trial. It seems that someone has stolen the Queen's tarts (small pies or cakes). Alice can see that the trial is full of nonsense, just like everything else in this strange place. She begins to grow again and decides to stand up to the Queen, who threatens to cut off her head.

Alice, now at full size, shouts, "You're nothing but a pack of cards!" The cards rise into the air and attack, fluttering down around her . . .

And then Alice wakes up. She is safe on her sister's lap by the bank of the river. It had all been a weird and wonderful dream.

CHAPTER 4
Readers Want More!

In 1865, booksellers in England stocked their shelves with Charles Dodgson's *Alice's Adventures in Wonderland*. It sold well—about five hundred copies in the first three weeks. England's Queen Victoria enjoyed the book so much that she asked Charles Dodgson to be sure to send her a copy of his next one! Charles collected newspaper reviews in a scrapbook. Some reviews called him—writing as Lewis Carroll—a genius.

But not all readers liked the book. Some thought the story was strange and confusing. Books written for children up to this time either taught good manners or disguised lessons for children to learn within the stories. Charles's story about Alice did just the opposite. It made fun of strict rules. "I can guarantee," Charles later said, "that the books . . . do not teach anything at all."

The book did so well that new editions came out every year. *Wonderland* was successful beyond England. American readers also enjoyed it. By the end of 1869, it had been translated into German and French. Soon after, it was translated into Italian, Dutch, and Russian, too.

French translation of *Alice's Adventures in Wonderland*

Alice's Adventures in Wonderland was such a success that Charles wanted to create another story about Alice. John Tenniel agreed to draw the illustrations again. Charles wrote *Through the Looking-Glass and What Alice Found There*. It was published in December 1871. In only about a month, more than fifteen thousand eager readers had bought copies of Alice's next adventure.

In the first chapter of *Through the Looking-Glass*, Alice sits in a cozy chair on a cold winter day, watching her cat, Dinah, and two little kittens. She looks into the mirror (which people at that time called a looking glass) above the fireplace. Alice wishes she could visit the Looking-Glass House on the other side. She climbs up on a chair, and then onto the mantel. Before she knows it, she is on the other side of the glass!

In this opposite room, the red and white pieces from a game of chess are scattered all over the floor. Alice sees the Red Queen and King, the White Queen and King, and knights, pawns, and other game pieces walking and talking to one another!

Alice knows she should return home, but she is too curious! She wants to go outside. When she follows the path to the garden, it keeps

leading back to the house! After many tries, she finds the garden filled with talking flowers.

As Alice looks around this odd new place, she realizes that the land is divided into large squares. It is designed to be a giant chessboard! She meets the Red Queen, who grabs Alice's hand and runs with her over a great distance. But they end up under the same tree where they had started. Moving around this world confuses Alice a lot.

Alice's next adventure is in a train car filled with a strange mix of passengers—a man dressed in white paper, a horse, a goat, a beetle, and a tiny gnat. When the train suddenly fades away, only Alice and the gnat remain. Alice admits she is afraid of insects, so the gnat introduces her to some not-so-scary ones—a Rocking-horse-fly, Snap-dragon-fly, and Bread-and-Butterfly.

The next strange people she meets are the twins Tweedledum and Tweedledee. They look exactly the same—large round men dressed as schoolboys. They act like little boys, too.

When Tweedledee breaks his brother's rattle, Tweedledum gets very fussy. They agree to battle each other with an umbrella and a wooden sword. Alice tries to act like an adult but can't help laughing at their silliness.

She meets the White Queen, who seems to do everything backward—like crying before she pricks her finger instead of after. Everything in this Looking-Glass world seems impossible.

The White Queen reassures Alice that impossible things are normal here. "Sometimes I've believed as many as six impossible things before breakfast," the Queen says.

Of course, more impossible things happen! The Queen turns into a sheep, knitting with yarn, sitting behind the counter of a shop.

The knitting needles turn into oars, and the sheep and Alice then float along a stream. When the sheep asks Alice what she wants to buy, they end up back at the shop. Alice asks for an egg.

The shop grows into a forest, and Alice's egg grows larger and turns into the egg-shaped Humpty Dumpty. He has such a wide grin that she is afraid his head will fall off.

Humpty thinks he is much smarter than Alice, even though most of what he says doesn't make sense.

Alice hears a crash, and suddenly thousands of soldiers crowd the forest. A lion and unicorn are fighting. While they take a break, Alice serves them a plum cake. Next, the Red Knight gallops

up on his horse to take Alice prisoner. The White Knight comes to rescue her. The knights are so clumsy, they both fall off their horses again and again. In the end, the White Knight wins and takes Alice on a bumpy ride. She says she doesn't want to be a prisoner—she wants to be a queen.

When the White Knight delivers her to the correct chess square, Alice has a crown on her head. She sits between the Red Queen and the

White Queen. They tell her she has to pass a test before she can become a queen. They quiz her on math, languages, and science.

The queens disappear, and Alice is standing before a door marked "Queen Alice." When it opens, she enters a large hall filled with animal guests, all cheering and singing for her!

She sits between the Red and White Queens at the head of a table.

But the feast turns into a crazy scene. Candles grow to the ceiling like fireworks. The White Queen disappears into a bowl of soup. The Red Queen shrinks to the size of a doll and runs around the table. Alice picks up the tiny queen and . . .

The Red Queen turns into a little kitten. Alice is back on her own side of the looking glass, at home in front of the fireplace. Like in *Alice's Adventures in Wonderland, Through the Looking-Glass* ends with Alice realizing all her fun has been just a dream.

Secret Messages

Charles Dodgson added lots of secret messages to the Liddell family in his Alice stories.

- In *Wonderland*, Alice's adventures down the rabbit hole begin on May 4. This was Alice Liddell's birthday.

- Charles uses the names of all the Liddell daughters in his books. Alice is named after Alice Liddell. In *Wonderland*, he named the Lory (a type of parrot) for Lorina and the Eaglet for Edith. In *Through the Looking-Glass*, the youngest Liddell sisters, Rhoda and Violet, are the talking flowers Rose and Violet.

- The Dodo and the Duck are named for Dodgson and Duckworth. Because Charles had a stutter, and sometimes pronounced his own last name "Do-Do-Dodgson."

- At the very end of *Through the Looking-Glass*, Charles includes an acrostic poem. In an acrostic, the first letters of each line spell out a word (or words). In this case, the first letters spell out the words ALICE PLEASANCE LIDDELL.

CHAPTER 5
Alice for Everyone

Charles Dodgson was pleased that so many children and adults enjoyed his stories. He also wanted to reach even younger readers—those still in the "nursery." In Victorian times, the nursery was a group of rooms in a home set aside for children to sleep, eat, learn lessons, and play.

In 1889, Charles released a simple version of Alice's story called *The Nursery "Alice."* It began: "Once upon a time, there was a little girl called Alice: and she had a very curious dream."

In this edition, Tenniel's illustrations were in color. For the first time, readers saw Alice with blond hair, a blue bow, a yellow dress, blue stockings, and black shoes.

Alice went beyond books on December 23, 1886, at London's Prince of Wales Theatre. There, the actors performed *Alice in Wonderland: A Musical Dream-Play.* The first act of the play included scenes from *Wonderland* and the second act covered *Through the Looking-Glass.* Audiences were delighted! After more than fifty performances, the play went on tour to reach even more Alice fans.

The character of Alice was becoming so popular that companies started using Tenniel's illustrations of her, and those of the other Wonderland characters, to sell their products. People made Alice dolls, and put Alice's face on puzzles and card games. The characters even appeared in advertisements for products like soap and toothpaste!

A publisher in America released a copy of *Alice's Adventures in Wonderland* without Charles's permission in 1893. The illustrator, Thomas Crowell, changed the way Alice looked. Instead of the yellow dress Tenniel had given her in *The Nursery "Alice,"* Crowell gave her a blue one.

Charles Dodgson died in 1898. The character of Alice would live far longer in the pages of his books. At the time of his death, *Alice's Adventures in Wonderland* had sold more than 150,000 copies, and *Through the Looking-Glass* 100,000. When Charles died, one of his brothers wrote to Alice Liddell, who had since been married to Reginald Hargreaves and had children of her own. He had found photographs in Charles's rooms at Oxford and sent them to Alice to remind her of how special she had been to his brother,

the author known around the world as Lewis Carroll.

By the end of the 1800s, Victorian rules had become less strict. Children were encouraged to use their imaginations more. They dressed up, had tea parties, and played with toy soldiers. They pretended to be fairies, giants, elves, and other fantastical creatures that they read about in books like those about Alice. Charles's stories inspired other authors to write about characters visiting new make-believe worlds. The American author L. Frank Baum's tale *The Wonderful Wizard of*

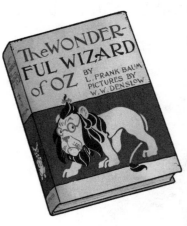

Oz is similar to Alice's story. Baum's character, Dorothy, meets many strange new creatures in a strange new land called Oz, then returns safe and sound to her home at the end.

Even though Charles Dodgson had died, other authors still wanted to tell Alice's story. In 1907 alone, more than thirteen new editions were published! Over time, authors made up their own Alice stories set in places such as Happyland, Monsterland, and Motorland. From 1905 to 1911, the comic strip *Little Nemo in Slumberland* ran in the *New York Herald* newspaper. In each weekly strip, a boy named Nemo falls asleep and dreams a new adventure, just like Alice did.

L. Frank Baum (1856–1919)

The American children's author Lyman Frank Baum was born in Chittenango, New York. He never finished high school. Instead, he worked and spent time acting in and writing plays. He did some writing for newspapers, but when he was forty, he decided to write for children.

In 1900, Baum's *The Wonderful Wizard of Oz* was published. Before this time, American children mostly read books by English authors, such as Lewis Carroll (Charles Dodgson). But Baum was the first successful American author of books for children. In much the way Dodgson wanted to delight children with *Alice's Adventures in Wonderland*, Baum said that he wrote his book not to teach lessons but just for fun.

In Baum's story, Dorothy Gale, a young girl from Kansas, and her dog, Toto, get swept up in a tornado and dropped into the land of Oz. Dorothy makes friends with the Tin Woodman, the Scarecrow, and the Cowardly Lion. She battles against the Wicked Witch of the West and her flying monkeys. To leave Oz, Dorothy clicks her shoes together and returns to Kansas.

Baum's idea turned into a series. He went on to write thirteen more books about Oz.

CHAPTER 6
Alice Goes to the Movies

The earliest movies were silent, black-and-white, and short. Two Alice movies made in 1903 (*Alice in Wonderland*) and 1910 (*Alice's Adventures in Wonderland*) were each only about ten minutes long. Readers of the books imagined Wonderland as a funny and fabulous place. But because movie technology was so new, it was hard for filmmakers to make Wonderland look wonderful.

In 1915, filmmaker W. W. Young directed a longer version of *Alice in Wonderland*. The character Alice was played by a fifteen-year-old actress named Viola Savoy. The movie had music for its soundtrack and no other sound. Viola had to act out how she felt without using words.

The odd creatures of Wonderland, such as the White Rabbit, the Cheshire Cat, and the Caterpillar, were actors in costumes that were modeled after Tenniel's original illustrations.

Viola Savoy as Alice

Sound had arrived for movies by the time a 1931 version of *Alice in Wonderland* was released. But the noises made by the camera could be heard throughout the entire movie! The most successful early version of *Alice in Wonderland* was released by the major studio Paramount in 1933. Directed by Norman Z. McLeod, the movie had almost fifty cast members, including some very famous actors at the time: W. C. Fields played Humpty Dumpty, Cary Grant played the Mock Turtle, and Gary Cooper played the White Knight. The studio auditioned seven thousand girls around the world to find just the right Alice! They hired an unknown seventeen-year-old actress named Charlotte Henry.

Actor Cary Grant with his Mock Turtle costume, 1933

In this movie, the sets, costumes, and special effects were more detailed and effective in bringing the imaginative world of Wonderland to life.

Alice was also the main character of the first movies made by Walt Disney. During his life,

Walt created Mickey Mouse, opened amusement parks, and started a worldwide entertainment corporation. But it was Alice who helped start his career.

As a young boy in Missouri in the early 1900s, Walt liked to draw. As he grew older, he discovered animation. Animation was a new art form at the time. When drawn pictures were shown quickly together, they looked like they were moving.

Young Walt Disney

He wanted to make a seven-minute movie with one of his favorite childhood characters—Alice! For his 1923 film *Alice's Wonderland*, he would combine animation (drawings) with a live person on-screen. Walt asked four-year-old Virginia Davis to play Alice. He had no money to pay the young actress, but her parents still agreed.

Virginia Davis

In the film, a curious Alice knocks on the door of Walt's animation studio. She asks to see him draw his "funnies"—his cartoon drawings. She is amazed as his pictures come to life on the page! That night, after her mother tucks her into bed, she has a dream. In it, she arrives by train in Cartoonland. All sorts of animals await her arrival! Mice, monkeys, dogs, hippos, cats, giraffes, flamingos, and more hold banners, wave signs, and cheer and clap when she steps off the train. They hold a parade in her honor. Alice rides an elephant and waves to the crowd.

Then trouble arrives! Lions escape from their cage and chase Alice down a rabbit hole! She escapes but finds herself at the edge of a cliff. When she leaps off, she falls down, down, down, and then . . . wakes up from her dream.

Walt barely had any money, but he worked

hard to complete the movie. He even slept in his office and took baths at the train station because he couldn't afford an apartment. *Alice's Wonderland* was never released in theaters. But it was the start of Walt Disney's road to success when he moved to Hollywood.

CHAPTER 7
Short and Long Alice Adventures

When Walt Disney moved to Hollywood, California, in 1923, he started an animation studio with his brother Roy. One of their first big projects was to make a whole series of short Alice films called *Alice Comedies*. Walt wrote to Virginia Davis's mother and asked them to come to California so Virginia could play Alice once again.

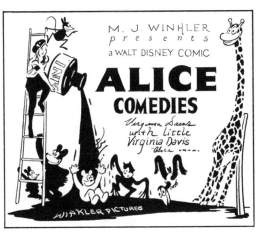

Walt filmed Virginia in an empty lot. He placed her in front of a large piece of white fabric and said, "Let's pretend!" He told her to act frightened or to look upset, even though she was all alone on the set. After shooting, he went back to his studio and added the cartoon characters in the white space around the actress.

The first *Alice Comedy* was called *Alice's Day at Sea*. Next came *Alice's Spooky Adventure* and *Alice's Wild West Show*. The short silent films were not much like the original Alice books at all. The *Alice Comedies* were first shown in theaters in early 1924, and by the end of the year, they were playing in theaters all over the United States.

Over the four-year run of the films, the actress Virginia Davis was replaced by Dawn O'Day; Margie Gay then followed, and finally Lois Hardwick. Partway through the series, Walt added a cat named Julius to join Alice on her adventures. In all, Disney produced fifty-six short *Alice Comedies* between 1924 and 1927.

Julius

After making many short cartoons, Walt started making full-length animated movies. No one had ever done that before. They weren't certain that audiences would want to watch a cartoon for an hour or more. Walt's success with *Snow White and the Seven Dwarfs* in 1937 proved that they did. For almost twenty years, he had wanted to work on a full-length Alice movie. Finally he was able to turn his attention to the character that had started his successful career.

Ten-year-old Kathryn Beaumont was hired to play Alice. She provided Alice's gentle voice. Even though the movie would be animated, Kathryn also acted out scenes. The animators in the room drew sketches of Kathryn's actions and expressions to inspire their final drawings of Alice's character. As an adult, Kathryn Beaumont said that being Alice was one of the highlights of her life.

The decision about how Alice would look had a lot to do with the art director and animator Mary Blair. Her artwork was bright and bold. The animators followed her direction to finalize the look of Wonderland in the Disney movie.

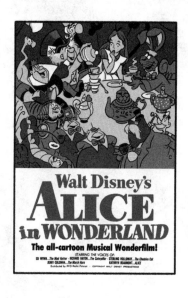

The studio chose parts from *Alice's Adventures in Wonderland* and *Through the Looking-Glass* to tell Alice's story. It also added music to help the story along. Songs such as "I'm Late," sung by the White Rabbit, and "All in the Golden Afternoon,"

sung by Alice and the flowers, made the movie complete.

Walt Disney's *Alice in Wonderland* didn't make a lot of money when it was released in 1951. But it is now a classic. It also created one of the most memorable images we have of Alice.

Mary Blair (1911–1978)

Mary Blair was born in Oklahoma in 1911. She began her career as an animator in the film industry, and in 1940 started to work for Walt Disney Studios. She worked there at a time when most of the animators were men.

In 1941, after a long trip to South America, Mary's style started to include bright bold flat shapes and colors. Walt realized her style would be perfect for his movie about Alice.

Mary left the Disney studio to work as an illustrator. Over the years, she drew many pictures for the famous children's series of Golden Books.

Walt invited Mary to help design the It's a Small World ride for the 1964 World's Fair in New York City. The ride was so popular that it became a featured attraction at Disney's amusement parks.

CHAPTER 8
Alice Everywhere

Alice is such a popular character that writers and artists kept retelling her story throughout the twentieth century and into the twenty-first. Publishers have released more than 7,500 editions of books about her. Each one reinvents Alice in its own way.

Salvador Dalí, a famous Spanish artist, created twelve illustrations for a 1969 edition of *Alice's Adventures in Wonderland*. They are dreamlike swirls of colors and lines, like the dreamy feeling of the original story. They are

One of Salvador Dalí's *Wonderland* prints

called his *Wonderland* prints.

Readers can see how much Alice has changed from 1865 with a 1999 edition of *Alice's Adventures in Wonderland* by Helen Oxenbury, an English children's book illustrator and writer. Her Alice is about as different from Tenniel's Alice as you can get! She does not wear the stiff dress and apron of Victorian times. Like any modern seven-year-old, she wears a comfortable tank dress and sneakers. She is ready for adventure.

Alice has even influenced popular cartoon characters on television. Scooby-Doo, the detective dog, falls asleep and dreams he is Alice in "Scooby in Wonderland." Dora the Explorer enters a mirror and has to follow her map to the queen's tea party in "Dora in Wonderland." Alice and the Care Bears enter Wonderland to keep an evil wizard from taking over in "The Care Bears Adventure in Wonderland." Hello Kitty plays Alice in a *Hello Kitty and Friends* version of *Alice in Wonderland*. Even *Sesame Street* made a version. *Abby in Wonderland* featured *Sesame Street* puppets in a retelling of the classic story.

Scene from "Scooby in Wonderland"

In the movies, director Tim Burton's 2010 *Alice in Wonderland* combined computerized special effects with live actors to create a very creepy world. His Alice is a teenager returning to Wonderland to defeat the Red Queen. Johnny Depp—the actor who played Captain Jack Sparrow in the *Pirates of the Caribbean* movies and Willy Wonka in *Charlie and the Chocolate Factory*—plays the Mad Hatter with fiery orange hair, bright green eyes, and an oversize polka-dot tie. In the sequel, *Alice Through the Looking Glass*, Alice returns to Wonderland to help the Mad Hatter.

Johnny Depp as the Mad Hatter

The television network ABC created a family television show called *Once Upon a Time in Wonderland* in 2013. In the series, everyone thinks Alice is crazy. She has to prove to them that her stories of Wonderland are true, so she goes back there to save her lost love.

Alice has not only inspired movies and television shows. She has also been important to the fashion industry. In 2015, American fashion designer Marc Jacobs (inspired by Disney's Alice) launched an eighty-piece collection called I Am Not Like Other Girls. It was stylish and silly. Images of the colorful garden of talking flowers decorated jewelry, bags, and sweatshirts. Some were covered in googly eyes! In 2016, Alice-themed makeup hit the stores from the company Urban Decay. The kit included eye shadows and lipsticks, with names like Heads Will Roll, Reflection, Gone Mad, and Dream On.

I Am Not Like Other Girls collection by Marc Jacobs

Children and adult fans alike buy or make Alice costumes to wear on Halloween. And of course, they throw tea parties! Many restaurants serve afternoon tea, a British tradition, with an Alice theme. At home, people host their own

Mad Tea Parties. Food plays a big part in *Alice's Adventures in Wonderland,* so there are many menu choices—mushrooms, tarts, and drinks labeled "Drink Me."

CHAPTER 9
Visiting Wonderland

Alice fans find plenty of adventure on themed amusement park rides. On Disneyland California's *Alice in Wonderland* ride, guests board a caterpillar-shaped car and move along tracks down the rabbit hole. They pass through the garden of singing flowers, the crazy croquet game, and the Mad Tea Party. Screens and moving figures called animatronics bring the story to life. In Florida's Disney World and Tokyo Disneyland, the teacup rides take guests on a spin that is dizzying—like Alice must have felt at the Mad Tea Party! At Shanghai Disneyland and Disneyland Paris, park guests can wander through hedge mazes that have an Alice theme.

Amusement parks aren't the only places to find Alice. Visitors to New York City's Central Park can see a sculpture of Alice, along with the Mad Hatter and the White Rabbit. The eleven-foot-tall bronze tribute was created in 1959. Alice, sitting on top of a giant mushroom, looks like the character in Tenniel's original illustrations. Children are encouraged to climb

up to get close to this larger-than-life Alice. Another famous Alice statue stands in the Alice Garden at Guildford Castle in England. Guildford is the town where Charles Dodgson wrote *Through the Looking-Glass*. The sculpture, erected in 1990, shows Alice reaching through a mirror, halfway between one world and the other.

Important religious people are often shown in stained-glass windows of churches. And Alice is right up there with them. The stained-glass window in the Great Hall of Christ Church in Oxford, England, includes an image of Alice Liddell. Another stained-glass window linking to Alice can be found in the All Saints Church in Daresbury, the town in Cheshire, England, where Charles was born. This one shows both Charles and the character Alice, as well as other characters from the books.

Tourists in England can take a river ride on the same route that Alice Liddell and Charles Dodgson took back in 1862. On the boat, guests drink tea and nibble treats, just like the Liddell girls did on their picnic. Also in England, the British Museum in London holds the most important piece of Alice's tale—the original story itself! Charles's handwritten and drawn copy of *Alice's Adventures Under Ground* is kept there.

Love for Alice has spread to all parts of the world. Japan has many Alice-themed restaurants. Alice ballets are performed in Sydney, Australia.

The Real Alice Story

Unlike the seven-year-old character Alice, Alice Liddell didn't stay a child forever! She grew up, married Reginald Hargreaves, and had three sons. She held on to the copy of *Alice's Adventures Under Ground* that Charles had made for her until 1928, when she was in her seventies. She sold it for 15,400 British pounds, which is almost $2 million today!

There were times when Alice Hargreaves found it hard to be known as the original Alice. Fans were always taking her picture or asking for interviews. She once wrote her son, "Oh, my dear I am tired of being Alice in Wonderland!" In 1932, which would have been the year that marked Charles Dodgson's one hundredth birthday, Alice Hargreaves came to New York from England. She was eighty years old. "Alice in U.S. Land!" the news reported. She stayed in expensive hotels and was given awards and treated to celebrations in her honor.

Alice Hargreaves, the original Alice, died in 1934 at the age of eighty-two.

The Netherlands holds Alice festivals. On the island of New Zealand, the Larnach family, who lived during Charles's time and loved the books, planted an Alice garden around their castle. The parents even named their own daughter Alice.

Of course, fans can always visit Wonderland in the pages of Alice's books. Over the past 150 years since *Alice's Adventures in Wonderland* was first published, the book has been translated into more than 170 languages. Blind people can read it in braille, a system in which raised dots stand for letters. There is a version of the story written in emojis to be read on smartphones!

Alice's story has changed over time in many ways. Although she is more than 150 years old in print, Alice will always be a brave, curious, and adventurous young girl.

Bibliography

*Books for young readers

All Saints Church Daresbury, England. "Lewis Carroll Window."
https://daresburycofe.org.uk/about-us/lewis-carroll-
window.

Brooker, Will. *Alice's Adventures: Lewis Carroll in Popular
Culture*. New York: Continuum, 2004.

Burton, Tim, dir. *Alice in Wonderland*. Walt Disney Pictures, 2010.

Carroll, Lewis. *Alice's Adventures Under Ground*. British Library.
Original manuscript: 186264. www.bl.uk/collection-items/
alices-adventures-under-ground-the-original-manuscript-
version-of-alices-adventures-in-wonderland.

*Carroll, Lewis. *Alice's Adventures in Wonderland, Through the
Looking Glass*. New York: Puffin Books, 1978.

CentralPark.com "Alice in Wonderland."
https://www.centralpark.com/things-to-do/attractions/
alice-in-wonderland/.

Douglas-Fairhurst, Robert. *The Story of Alice: Lewis Carroll and
the Secret History of Wonderland*. Cambridge, MA: The
Belknap Press of Harvard University Press, 2015.

Gabler, Neal. *Walt Disney: The Triumph of the American
Imagination*. New York: Alfred A. Knopf, 2006.

Gardner, Martin, and Mark Burstein, eds. *The Annotated Alice:
150th Anniversary Deluxe Edition*. New York: W. W. Norton &
Company, 2015.

Geronimi, Clyde, Wilfred Jackson, and Hamilton Luske, dirs. *Alice in Wonderland*. Walt Disney Productions, 1951.

Hunt, Peter, ed. *Children's Literature: An Illustrated History*. Oxford, England: Oxford University Press, 1995.

Meigs, Cornelia et al. *A Critical History of Children's Literature*. London: The Macmillan Company, 1969.

Mynott, Nicole. "Take a Peek at the Marc by Marc Jacobs Alice in Wonderland Collection." Disney/Style. style.disney.com/ fashion/2015/10/29/take-a-peek-at-the-marc-by-marc-jacobs-alice-in-wonderland-collection/.

Phillips, Robert, ed. *Aspects of Alice: Lewis Carroll's Dreamchild as Seen Through the Critics' Looking-Glasses*. New York: Vanguard Press, 1971.

*Pollack, Pam, and Meg Belviso. *Who Was Lewis Carroll?* New York: Penguin Workshop, 2017.

Popova, Maria. "The Best Illustrations from 150 Years of Alice in Wonderland." Brain Pickings. www.brainpickings.org/2014/07/07/best-illustrations-alice-in-wonderland/.